Gardening Guides

Indoor Gardening

GROWING AIR PLANTS, TERRARIUMS, AND MORE

by Lisa J. Amstutz

CAPSTONE PRESS
a capstone imprint

Snap Books are published by Capstone Press,
1710 Roe Crest Drive, North Mankato, Minnesota 56003
www.mycapstone.com

Library of Congress Cataloging-in-Publication Data
Amstutz, Lisa J., author.
 Indoor gardening : growing air plants, terrariums, and more / Lisa Amstutz.
   pages cm. — (Snap books. Gardening guides)
 Audience: Ages 8–14.
 Audience: Grades 4 to 6.
 Summary: "Provides readers with gardening projects that can be done
indoors"—Provided by publisher.
 Includes bibliographical references and index.
 ISBN 978-1-4914-8236-0 (library binding)
 ISBN 978-1-4914-8626-9 (eBook PDF)
 1. Indoor gardening—Juvenile literature. I. Title.
  SB419.A47 2016
  635.9'65—dc23
                              2015031203

Editorial Credits
Abby Colich, editor; Bobbie Nuytten and Tracy McCabe, designers;
Tracy Cummins and Morgan Walters, media researchers;
Laura Manthe, production specialist

Image Credits
All photographs by Capstone Studio: Karon Dubke with the exception of:
Shutterstock: Andrey_Kuzmin (Soil), Antonova Anna, Back Cover,
asharkyu, Back Cover, 19 (Cactus), Nenov Brothers Images, 25, Tanee, 5, 14-15,
Zoom Team, 30-31
Design Elements by Shutterstock

Printed in Canada.
102015   009223FRS16

Table of Contents

Gardening Indoors 4

Water Garden 6

"Spice It Up" Garden. 8

Pocket Garden. 10

Desert Garden 12

Spring Beauties 14

Teacup Garden 16

A Garden of Words 18

Flytrap Garden 20

Air Garden 22

Zen Garden 24

Bonsai Garden. 26

Living Wall Art 28

Solving Plant Problems. 30

Read More. 32

Internet Sites. 32

Gardening Indoors

No matter where you live, you can create fabulous gardens indoors. It doesn't take a green thumb to grow these gardens—just some sunshine and daily care. Gardening is a great way to express your artistic flair and brighten up your home.

Each project in this book includes a list of the materials you'll need. Most can be found at a nursery, department store, or hardware store. But if you can't find the exact plants or supplies listed, don't despair. Use what you can find and give the project your own twist.

Indoor gardens are easy to care for. Water houseplants whenever the soil feels dry below the surface. Poke your finger into the soil to check. Many of the projects in this book will simply require you to use a spray bottle to mist the plants with water.

It's a good idea to add some fertilizer to your soil or water every month or two. Buy liquid houseplant fertilizer or plant spikes, and follow the directions on the package. It's also a good idea to wipe the leaves of plants with a soft damp cloth whenever they start to look dusty.

Eventually, a plant may grow too large for its pot. If this happens, carefully remove the plant, gently loosen the roots, and replant it in a larger container. Fill in around it with fresh potting soil.

If you care for your plants well, you can enjoy them for years to come. Ready, set, dig in!

WATERING TIP

Water your indoor plants with distilled water or rainwater. Tap water may contain chemicals and salts that will harm plants.

Water Garden

This simple but elegant water garden will dress up any room. Choose pebble colors to match your décor.

What You'll Need

- large clear bowl
- colorful glass pebbles or aquarium gravel
- rainwater or distilled water
- coffee anubias, water clover, and bamboo plants
- slow-release aquatic fertilizer capsule

Instructions

1. Place glass pebbles or gravel on the bottom of the bowl.

2. Set the anubias plant in the bowl. Layer pebbles over the roots to hold them in place.

3. Tuck the bamboo and water clover into the pebbles at the bottom of the bowl.

4. Fill the bowl with rainwater or distilled water. Leave a 2-inch (5-centimeter) space at the top. Set your water garden in a spot with indirect sunlight.

5. To care for your water garden, remove any dead foliage you see. Add more water as it evaporates. Change it if it becomes smelly or discolored.

6. Each spring add a slow-release aquatic fertilizer capsule to the water to feed your plants.

INDIRECT SUNLIGHT

For plants that thrive in indirect sunlight, pull down a shade during the sunniest part of the day. Or move the plant a few feet away from the window when the sun is at its brightest.

MORE PLANT OPTIONS

If you can't find the plants listed, try any of these in your water garden.

- java moss
- hornwort
- water pennywort
- dwarf baby's tears
- micro sword

"Spice It Up" Garden

"Terra" means earth or land. Create your own miniature world, or terrarium, using empty spice jars. Group several on a windowsill or table for a pretty display. The lid on the jar helps keep moisture around the plants.

What You'll Need

- clear spice jars with lids
- small stones or glass pebbles
- potting soil
- twigs, small shells, acorn caps, bark, or other natural items
- skewer or chopstick
- baby's tears plants
- moss (If you use dried moss, soak for three hours before using.)

Instructions

1. Wash spice jars well, and remove any labels. If a label won't come off easily, soak the jar in hot water to soften the glue.

2. Place pebbles in the bottom of each jar. Add about 1.5 inches (3.8 cm) of potting soil.

3. Use the skewer to poke holes in the potting soil. Insert baby's tears into the holes.

4. Tuck moss around the plants with the skewer.

5. Decorate with a few natural items.

6. Use a clean spray bottle to mist the soil with water.

7. Put the lids on the jars and set them on a sunny windowsill.

8. Lightly mist the plants with a clean spray bottle every 3 to 4 weeks to keep the soil moist. If a jar fogs up, remove the lid for a few hours to let some of the moisture evaporate.

TERRARIUM TIPS

- *If you don't have a spice container, try a baby food jar or other small clear jar with a lid.*
- *Other good plants to try are ground clover and micro mini sinningia.*
- *Consider painting the lids a color of your choice.*

Pocket Garden

Plant a pocket-sized garden in a candy
tin. This sweet little garden is small
enough to take anywhere!

What You'll Need

- small mint or candy tin
- small gravel
- cactus potting soil
- white stones
- zebra cactus, golden sedum, coppertone stonecrop, or other small succulent plants

Instructions

1. Put a single layer of gravel in the bottom of the tin.

2. Fill tin with potting soil.

3. Trim the stem of each plant so it is slightly shorter than the height of the tin. Push stem of one plant into the soil. Press soil around it to hold it in place. Repeat for each plant.

4. Add stones on top of the soil.

5. Lightly mist plants with a clean spray bottle two to three times per week in spring and summer. Water once a month in fall and winter.

Desert Garden

Do you have trouble remembering to water your houseplants?
Then this is the garden for you. These plants like it dry!

What You'll Need

- small, shallow flowerpots with holes for drainage
- gravel
- cactus potting soil mix
- funnel
- sand
- leather or nylon gloves
- rose pincushion cactus, globe cactus,
  lipstick echeveria (also called "red edge"),
  or any other small cacti or succulents

Instructions

1. Place a layer of gravel in the bottom of each pot.

2. Mix one part potting soil and one part sand. Fill each pot halfway.

3. Wearing gloves, set one plant on top of each pot. Add more potting soil and sand mixture around them, pressing gently in place. Handle with care. Cactus spines are sharp!

4. Top each pot with a thin layer of sand. Use a funnel to spread the sand so it doesn't collect on the cactus spines.

5. Set your cactus garden in a warm, sunny spot.

6. Water your cacti once a week during the spring and summer. Set the pots in a shallow dish of water—about 1 inch (2.5 cm)—until the surface is moist. Then take them out to drain. Water once a month in fall and winter.

COLORFUL GARDEN

For a colorful desert garden variation, use colored sand in a clear container. Or try painting your pots with nontoxic paints in warm earth tones such as orange, red, yellow, and sage green.

Spring Beauties

Can't wait for spring? Plant a pot of cheerful spring bulbs. Chill the bulbs to "force," or trick, them into blooming early.

What You'll Need

- flowerpots, 4 inches (10 cm) in diameter
- nontoxic paints
- paintbrush
- potting soil
- 4 daffodil, hyacinth, or tulip bulbs (Choose dwarf varieties if possible.)

Instructions

1. Paint the pots in colors and designs of your choosing. Let paint dry overnight.

2. Fill each pot halfway with potting soil. Set bulbs on top, pointed ends up.

3. Add more soil until just the tip of each bulb is showing. Water them well. Repeat for each pot.

4. Place the pots in a refrigerator or cold garage for 8 to 10 weeks.

5. Take the pots out, and put in a dark closet for a week or two until the bulbs begin to sprout.

6. Set the pots in a sunny window. Water two to three times per week or as needed.

7. Once the plants finish blooming and the leaves die, brush the dirt off the bulbs and let them dry. Place them between layers of newspaper in a cardboard box or paper bag and store in a cool, dry place. (A closet or cold garage works well.) Replant the next year.

FLOWERPOT TIP

If a pot has holes in the bottom for drainage, set it in a saucer to collect the water. This will also keep water from damaging the surface under the pot.

Teacup Garden

Tuck some miniature ivy into a dainty teacup. You can find inexpensive teacups at thrift stores or yard sales. Arrange several of these tiny gardens on a tray for an elegant display.

What You'll Need

- teacups with matching saucers
- masking tape
- drill
- small gravel
- potting soil
- select from the following for each teacup: miniature ivy, baby's tears, "mini white" mosaic plant, oregano, or stonecrop

Instructions

1. Make an X on the bottom of each teacup with masking tape. Have an adult drill a hole in the center of each X.

2. Put a thin layer of gravel in the bottom of each teacup.

3. Fill one teacup half full of potting soil. Set a plant inside, then fill in soil around it, leaving 1 inch (2.5 cm) of space at the top. Press soil firmly to hold the plant in place. Repeat for each teacup.

4. Place each teacup on its saucer and set on a sunny windowsill.

5. Using a clean spray bottle, mist plants with water daily.

HOUSEPLANT FACT

Did you know that houseplants help clean the air in your home? They put oxygen into the air when they breathe and can also remove pollutants.

A Garden of Words

Have an old book sitting around? Here's a novel idea. Instead of throwing it away, turn it into a garden. Succulents are a good choice for book gardens because they don't need much water.

What You'll Need

- ✎ old book at least 2 inches (5 cm) thick
- ✎ white glue
- ✎ metal ruler
- ✎ pencil
- ✎ utility knife
- ✎ parchment paper or plastic bag
- ✎ cactus potting soil
- ✎ small, smooth stones
- ✎ 2 to 3 small succulents, such as an *Echeveria* species or stonecrop

Instructions

1. Drizzle white glue over the page edges and spread it around with your fingers. Let it dry thoroughly. This will hold the pages together.

2. With a ruler and pencil, mark a rectangle in the center of the first page of the book. This may be 4 to 6 inches (10 to 15 cm) wide, depending on the size of your book.

3. Have an adult use the utility knife to cut out the rectangle, removing a few pages at a time. Keep removing the cut pages and cutting the next layer until the hole is at least 1.5 inches (3.8 cm) deep.

4. Line the hole with parchment paper or plastic bag and fill with soil.

5. Poke holes in the soil with pencil and insert the plants. Press soil around them to hold them in place.

6. Cover remaining soil with small, smooth stones.

7. Mist the garden thoroughly with a clean spray bottle.

8. Trim away any plastic or parchment that sticks out.

9. During spring and summer, mist the plants with water once a week. Be careful not to get the book wet. Water once a month in fall and winter.

Flytrap Garden

You've heard of animals that eat plants—but the other way around? That's right. These carnivorous plants love to eat flies! The insects are attracted to the plant's scent. They crawl inside, only to be trapped and slowly digested.

What You'll Need

- glass jar or bowl with a small opening at the top
- small stones or aquarium gravel
- clean, coarse sand
- dry sphagnum moss (Soak in water for an hour before using.)
- Venus flytrap plant

FLYTRAP FACT

Venus flytraps live in forests where the air is warm and damp. They can survive in poor soil because they get nutrients from the insects they eat.

FLYTRAP CARE

A Venus flytrap will not close its leaves unless it is hungry. You can check if it is hungry by touching the leaves. But don't trigger the leaves too often. You may stress the plant.

Instructions

1. Put a layer of stones in the bottom of the glass jar or bowl.

2. Mix one part sand to two parts sphagnum moss. Add to the pot.

3. Poke holes in the moss and sand mixture with your finger. Set the Venus flytrap plant inside. Press firmly to hold it in place.

4. Water soil thoroughly.

5. Set your pot in a warm place with indirect sunlight. In warm weather set it outdoors in partial shade.

6. Use clean spray bottle to mist plant daily or as needed to keep the soil moist.

7. Be sure your Venus flytrap eats about once a month. It can eat a live fly or tiny piece of raw meat about the size of a fly.

Air Garden

These amazing plants don't need any soil at all! Air plants can grow almost anywhere. In their natural rain forest environment, they grow on other plants. They take in water and nutrients through their leaves.

What You'll Need

- 8-inch (20-cm) square picture frame
- nontoxic paint
- paintbrush
- at least 12 heavy staples or hooks
- hammer
- fishing line or embroidery floss
- 3 air plants (any *Tillandsia* species)
- foliar fertilizer (Purchase at a nursery or order online.)

Instructions

1. Remove backing from the frame. Turn it over. Have an adult help you push or hammer the staples or hooks into the back or inside of the frame. Do not push them all the way in. You will need enough space to string the fishing line or floss underneath.

2. Paint your frame. Let it dry overnight.

3. Tie one end of the fishing line or floss to a staple or hook. Then string it randomly through the remaining staples or hooks to create interesting angles.

4. Tuck your air plants into spots where the string crosses.

5. Hang your frame in a warm place away from direct sunlight.

6. Using a clean spray bottle, mist plants 2 to 3 times per week. Every 2 to 3 weeks, take them out of the frame and soak entire plants in a bowl of water for a half hour. Shake the water off and put them back into the frame.

7. Remove dead leaves and make sure water does not collect at the base of the plant.

8. Spray once a month with foliar fertilizer to provide nutrients.

AIR PLANT FACT

Plants that grow on other plants without harming them are called epiphytes. They get the water and nutrients they need from the air and the plant debris that collects around them.

MORE OPTIONS

Try growing air plants in seashells, driftwood, or small jars.

Zen Garden

Create swirling designs in sand with this soothing Zen garden. Then smooth out the sand and start again. Zen gardens are an ancient Japanese tradition. They are designed to help the mind focus and meditate.

What You'll Need

- wide, shallow tray or pot
- small shallow container (a tuna or sardine can will work)
- hammer and nail
- gravel
- cactus potting soil mix
- sand
- fork
- a few smooth pebbles, pieces of driftwood, seashells, or other natural items
- small jade plant

Instructions

1. Have an adult help you poke three drainage holes in the small container with hammer and nail.

2. Add a layer of gravel to the small container.

3. Set jade plant in the container and fill in around it with soil. Press soil firmly to hold it in place.

4. Fill pot or tray with smooth sand.

5. Set the small container on the sand and press gently into the sand.

6. Add a few smooth rocks, pieces of driftwood, or shells in a pleasing arrangement.

7. Use a fork or stick to draw wavy lines or make patterns in the sand. Place garden in a sunny spot.

8. Use a clean spray bottle to mist twice a week during the spring and summer. Water once a month in fall and winter.

PLANTLESS GARDEN

You can make a Zen garden without any plants at all! Simply arrange a dish of sand and natural items to create pleasing patterns. This version of a Zen garden is great for those have trouble remembering to water their plants.

MORE PLANT OPTIONS

If you don't have a jade plant, try one of these:

- Aeonium domesticum
- Echeveria agavoides
- Aloe vera
- *mother of pearl*
- *sedum*

Bonsai Garden

Bonsai is Chinese for "tree in a pot." The art of bonsai began about 1,800 years ago in China. It then spread to Japan. This ancient art is still alive and well today. Try growing your own miniature tree in a pot. Trim your bonsai carefully to keep it small.

What You'll Need

- shallow 6-inch (15-cm) diameter pot with drainage holes
- gravel
- potting soil
- moss
- small ficus plant (tiger bark, Green Island, willow leaf fig, or Chinese banyan)

Instructions

1. Place gravel in the bottom of the container or pot.

2. Fill with potting soil to within 3 inches (7.6 cm) of the rim.

3. Set your ficus plant in the pot. Fill in around it with potting soil to 1 inch (2.5 cm) below the rim. Press soil firmly around the plant to hold it in place.

4. Add moss around the plant to cover the bare soil. Press it gently in place.

5. Check the soil every day. If it feels dry, set the pot in a shallow pan of water. Let it soak up as much water as it needs. Using a clean spray bottle, mist the leaves and moss with water once a day.

6. Trim the plant regularly. Repot into a larger container every two years, or if the roots start to come out the drainage holes.

HOW TO TRIM YOUR BONSAI

You can pinch back new shoots anytime, but do the major pruning in early spring or late fall.

1. Decide what shape and size you want the tree to be.

2. Remove shoots that stick out on the top and sides of the leaf canopy (the outer layer of leaves).

3. Remove some of the shoots inside the canopy so it doesn't get too crowded. Do not remove all the new growth.

4. Remove dead or dying leaves whenever you see them.

Living Wall Art

Hang a living picture! Arrange small succulents in a shadow box to create an interesting design.

What You'll Need

- wooden shadow box with glass removed, 5 x 7 inches (13 x 18 cm)
- picture frame with glass and cardboard backing removed, 5 x 7 inches (13 x 18 cm) (Look for these at thrift stores and garage sales.)
- nontoxic paint
- paintbrush
- piece of plastic, 9 x 11 inches (23 x 28 cm)
- scissors
- nails
- hammer
- hardware cloth with 0.5-inch (1.3-cm) grid
- staple gun with staples
- cactus potting soil
- moss
- pencil
- 3 hen and chicks, 2 *Echeveria*, and 2 sedum cuttings
- large hook or place to hang or display your garden

Instructions

1. Paint shadow box and frame with nontoxic paint. Let them dry overnight.

2. Trim succulent stems to about 2 inches (5 cm) long. Let them set out for a day or two to dry out.

3. Line the inside of the shadow box with plastic, and staple it in place.

4. Fill the box with soil and top with moss.

5. Cut hardware cloth to the size of your shadow box using the outside measurement. Staple it to the top of the shadow box.

6. Have an adult help you nail the picture frame to the top of the shadow box.

7. Poke a hole in the soil with a pencil. Plant one of the succulent stems. Add larger plants first. Then fill in with smaller ones to create a pattern.

8. Using a clean spray bottle, mist plants well with water. Lay the frame flat and keep it out of direct sunlight for two weeks, until the stems start to root.

9. Gradually move the frame to full sun. Have an adult help you hang it up. You can also prop it up against a wall.

10. Water your living frame once a month. Lay it flat, and thoroughly soak the soil. Let it drain well. Then rehang the frame.

Solving Plant Problems

To keep your houseplants happy, you need to mimic their natural growing conditions. That can be hard to do indoors. If your plants are showing signs of stress, they may be sending you a message. Learn to read these messages, and give plants what they need.

Pests

If your plant's leaves look curled, yellow, or webbed, your plant may have a pest problem. Check the leaves and stems carefully for insects or mites. If you find any, remove them with a tissue. You can also put a little dish soap and water in a spray bottle, and spray it on them.

Diseases

Dying leaves, powdery spots, and rotting roots can be signs of disease. Bacteria and fungi cause plant diseases. They often start when the plant is too damp. Remove any dead leaves, and avoid overwatering your plant. Keep water off the leaves, and make sure the plant has enough air circulation.

Other Problems

A plant with weak, spindly stems and leaves probably needs more light. Move it to a sunnier location.

Yellow leaves can mean that the plant needs more light, the soil is too wet, or the area is too cold or drafty. It may also need more fertilizer.

Wilted leaves are a sign that a plant is either too wet or dry. If the leaf tips turn brown, your water may be too soft, or the plant may need more water or warmth.

Scorched leaf tips mean the plant is getting too much direct sun. Move the plant to an area with less direct sunlight.

Read More

Brown, Renata Fossen. *Gardening Lab for Kids.* Hands-On Family. Beverly, Mass.: Quarry Books, 2014.

Cornell, Kari A. *The Nitty-Gritty Gardening Book: Fun Projects for All Seasons.* Minneapolis, Minn.: Millbrook Press, 2015.

Thomas, Isabel. *Experiments with Plants.* Read and Experiment. Chicago: Raintree, 2016.

Internet Sites

FactHound offers a safe, fun way to find Internet sites related to this book. All of the sites on FactHound have been researched by our staff.

Here's all you do:

Visit *www.facthound.com*

Type in this code: 9781491482360

 Check out projects, games and lots more at
www.capstonekids.com

Books in this series: